I0820373

Praise for *You Absolute Plonker*

"A most useful compendium—perfect for those occasions when civility fails and one must wound with style."

—Elizabeth Bennet

"For tongues too timid to wield daggers, this book shall teach them how."

—Lady Macbeth

"Deliciously rude! Like tea with vinegar—sharp, strange, filled with much muchness."

—The Mad Hatter

"Vile, vicious, and utterly divine! To anyone who hasn't read it, off with their heads!"

—The Queen of Hearts

"At last, a book that catalogues the pettiness of mankind with the elegance it scarcely deserves. I only wish the Yahoos could read."

–Lemuel Gulliver

"How thrilling! An entire book dedicated to clever cruelty—proof that language, like life, is best when unbuttoned."

—Bella Baxter

“Mediocrity knows nothing higher than itself, but talent instantly recognizes genius. And this clever book, my dear Watson, is nothing short of comedic brilliance.”

—Sherlock Holmes

“Every spy’s secret weapon is Agent Baker’s guide to verbal sharpshooting. Sure to leave your enemies shaken (not stirred), this handbook is a great tactical addition to any operative’s arsenal.”

—James Bond

“Whether jousting or jesting, no foe can best me with Excalibur at my hip and this tome by my side.”

—King Arthur

“Hark! For any saucy rapscallion who wishes to sharpen thy tongue, methinks this booketh is the finest whetstone of the wits. Better a witty fool than a foolish wit!”

—William Shakespeare

“I found this book in the Restricted Section, and I must insist upon caution for those who read it. Be sure to keep this volume out of the hands of Death Eaters, for these powerful spells will leave your opponents stupefied.”

—Hermione Granger

YOU ABSOLUTE PLONKER

YOU ABSOLUTE PLONKER

THE DEFINITIVE GUIDE TO BRITISH INSULTS

MICHAEL BAKER

Miami

Published by Mango Publishing, a division of Mango Publishing Group, Inc.

Cover Design: Elina Diaz
Cover Photo/illustration: Marina Zlochin/stock.adobe.com
Layout & Design: Elina Diaz

For permission requests, please contact the publisher at:
Mango Publishing Group
5966 South Dixie Highway, Suite 300
Miami, FL 33143
info@mango.bz

For special orders, quantity sales, course adoptions and corporate sales, please email the publisher at sales@mango.bz. For trade and wholesale sales, please contact Ingram Publisher Services at customer.service@ingramcontent.com or +1.800.509.4887.

You Absolute Plonker: The Definitive Guide to British Insults

Library of Congress Cataloging-in-Publication number: 2025943075
ISBN: (hc) 978-1-68481-871-6, (e) 978-1-68481-872-3
BISAC category code: HUM019000 HUMOR / Topic / Language

For my youngest daughter, Kymberley. My fiercest ally, my sharpest critic, and my #1 fan. You took an old man with a few good lines and made him a voice people wanted to hear. So, cheers to you, my darling girl. The daughter who made her father feel like a legend.

And for my beloved wife, Claudine. The first chapter, the foundation, the reason the rest was ever written.

With all my love,
Mike

Table of Contents

Introduction

Allow me to introduce myself. The name is Mike...Englishman Mike. A proud Brit with a tongue that could cut glass, and an unyielding love for British culture. I make it my business to translate the rituals of British small talk, workplace survival tactics, and culturally acceptable emotional repression to anyone mad enough to want to understand them. Do I believe sarcasm is the highest form of patriotism? Undoubtedly. To me, there is no intimacy without humour. And in Britain? Mockery is love. If I'm not taking the mickey out of you, are we even close?

Welcome to the uniquely charming world of British insults! In Britain, insulting someone is rarely just a matter of being rude; it's a national art form, perfected over centuries. Our jabs are often subtle, layered with wit, and delivered with just the right amount of propriety. We don't yell; we smirk. We don't curse at you; we suggest you might be a bit thick. This book is your ultimate guide to navigating the many colourful ways we Brits take the mickey out of each other. From the playful muppet to the more cutting gobshite, these insults are more than just words; they're a way of life. You'll find each insult paired with practical examples, so you can start using them in your everyday life. But remember, British insults are never meant to be taken too seriously. They're delivered with a wink, a nod, and very often, a cup of tea. Just remember: It's all in good fun. If your mate's never called you a prat, are you even mates? Now, put the kettle on. Let's get cheeky, shall we?

PART 1

What Makes an Insult Truly British?

There is something unique about a British insult that you'll never be able to replicate without first understanding the anatomy of the perfect zinger. First and foremost is the importance of understatement. We Brits are the supreme champions. Why be direct when you can vaguely allude to someone's incompetence? A Brit won't directly tell you your jumper looks like a cat threw up on it. Instead, we prefer the classics: "I wouldn't have chosen that, personally," or, "Well, that was brave." It cuts deeper because it's subtle. The second layer is polite framing. When crafting a clever British insult, one must remember to always keep it civil. So civil, in fact, that if you're not paying attention, the jab can be read as nearly a compliment! "You've really made that work for you!" or, "Oh, you're so confident wearing that." Devastating when properly understood, but wrapped in charm.

Moving on to sarcasm, but not just any sarcasm—sarcasm so dry, it's borderline dehydrated. A trademark of British humour, and British life, is that we often say the opposite of what we actually mean. The goal of this is to mock, tease, or point out something that is obviously ridiculous. Examples include "Well, aren't you clever" (translation: You are most definitely not clever), and "Lovely weather we're having" (when it's bucketing down outside). Bear in mind, dear readers, that delivery is everything. It's nearly always deadpan, meaning the punch is in the tone or context. The key here is to really understand your surroundings and make light of them. One really shouldn't let a perfectly absurd moment pass without a hilariously pointed observation.

Now, let's talk about the British knack for using inventive and absurd phrases in everyday life. As mentioned, a British insult is never mean-spirited. In fact, it's often meant to surprise and delight. Words like muppet and plonker are regularly used. You'll never hear a master of the British jab refer to you as ugly...no, no, that's frightfully bland. Instead, we'll say, "You've got a mug only a nan could love." If an insult lacks charm or wit, we simply don't bother. We're here to wound with style, not just because we like the sound of our own voices.

Right, now that you can properly use the word "muppet," let's quickly review class. The UK is famously obsessed with class, which is hardly surprising for a nation under sovereign rule for over a thousand years. This obsession is not only about money, but also manners, taste, accent, and even wardrobe. So naturally, our insults often target people's place (or attempted place) on the social ladder. You'll often hear comments in the realm of "It's a bit common, isn't it" (translation: It's tacky and I wouldn't be caught dead doing/wearing that), or "All fur coat and no knickers" (translation: Showy on the outside, nothing underneath).

Now that you understand the formula for crafting the perfect British zinger, let's discuss who this book is for. To put it bluntly? Absolutely everyone who has someone in their life who needs to be put in their place. This book is for the woman with the overbearing mother-in-law. She can't scream, so instead she says, "Oh, I didn't realise you were an expert in child psychology." It's for the office underdog, who is constantly talked over, undermined, and ignored. They can't rage-quit, so instead they say, "Do go on, I love to hear my ideas repeated back to me." This book belongs to the woman who is too classy to clap back, but too sharp to hold her tongue. She wants to win with wit. It's for the friend who is constantly one-upped by their peers. The ones who relentlessly have a better holiday, a more expensive car, or a house in a posher neighbourhood, and are in dire need of an "I do love how freely you hand out your unsolicited opinions."

The Importance of a Witty Insult

A witty insult is much more than a sharp jab; it's a social contract. There are a few reasons why this style of mockery is so beloved in Britain. First off, it's a mark of intelligence. Anyone can call someone an idiot. But a blithering idiot? That takes a touch more finesse. A witty insult lands because it's layered, unexpected, and sharp. It tells people that you are fast on your feet and know how to read a room. A witty insult isn't about attacking its victim; it's about entertaining the crowd. In British culture, it's a way to bond, not to bruise. It allows you to put someone in their place (rightfully so), but to do it with honesty and charm. Sometimes bad behaviour, stupidity, or pretension simply needs to be called out, but doing so bluntly can escalate a situation—and we wouldn't want that. A witty comeback softens the blow and lets everyone save face, even the recipient.

How to Use These Insults

Proceed with caution, as a well-delivered British insult packs a mighty punch. You can't just throw them around; you must know how to craft, as well as wield, this power. First off, know the difference between an insult and quick wit. A witty insult is playful and clever. It should make everyone in the room laugh, including your target. It's usually delivered in the form of an astute observation, not a harsh critique. Understand the difference between "You're a charming one, aren't you?" and "You are an idiot." One is sharp, but playful. The other is guaranteed to kill the mood. Pro tip: Stick to wit unless you're ready for an argument. In addition to wielding wit as a weapon, know your audience. Not every joke is for everyone. Are you among friends, where the remark will be well-received? Go forth and insult proudly! Are you at work, among colleagues and senior managers? Keep it subtle, or skip it altogether. The office is not the place for savage burns. Now that you know where and when to employ a jab, let's talk technique, because nothing ruins a good insult like poor execution.

Timing Is Everything

Especially when it comes to a verbal slap. Too early, and you're trying too hard. Too late, the moment is gone, and you'll come across like you're nursing a grudge. The perfect jab lands right after a brief pause, ideally when no one is expecting it. The sting is in the surprise. It should feel off-the-cuff, like you've just thought of it at that moment. Not like you've been waiting weeks to finally let that one out. A few key pointers to always keep in mind:

1. Don't double up on insults. Overdoing it kills the effect, and now you're more grinch, less comedic genius.
2. Let your face betray nothing. Laughing at your own joke is for amateurs. Keep it deadpan, keep it deadly.
3. Don't follow it up with an explanation, just let it sit. Let your silence do the damage. That's power. That's style. That's British.

Pair It with Charm and Humour

The key is to make your snark feel like banter. Start with a light smirk or grin on your face. Self-deprecating humour is your shield. If you mock yourself first, even a light roast, you earn the right to tease others. Humour helps the medicine go down. Exaggeration, irony, or absurd comparisons can make even a brutal line feel lighthearted. Compare someone's ego to a weather balloon, or their fashion sense to an experimental art exhibit. The point isn't just to insult; it's almost always to entertain.

Punch Up, Not Down

Punching up means that your insult is almost always aimed at someone with more power, status, social currency, or pompousness. We don't go after the underdog, the vulnerable, or the easy-to-embarrass. It's about targeting the deserving, not the defenceless. Punching up, when done correctly, can be viewed as charm because it feels cheeky, not cruel. It levels the playing field. It's why roasting the prime minister is allowed, but mocking the assistant is just plain mean.

Things to bear in mind:

1. **As the Royal Family says, never complain, never explain.** If your comedic prowess is lost on someone, and they ask, "Was that a dig?" simply smile and say, "Of course not." Let them figure it out. The jab should never be explained, lest we dilute the potency of the shade thrown.

2. **Subtle is the new savage.** Only a child goes for the direct punch. The British know how to keep it refined. Never say, "Your dress is hideous." Rather, try: "Oh my, that dress is quite interesting. I wish I had the courage to walk around town wearing that." Sharp, sophisticated, and cuts deeper than glass.

3. **Lean into formality.** This is one of the sharpest tools in the British-style insult toolkit, because nothing stings harder than being eviscerated politely. It's the equivalent of getting slapped with a cashmere glove: elegant, composed, and humbles you in a way that shouting never could. For example, you don't say, "He's lazy." You say, "He's mastered the art of selective

contribution." You don't say, "She's clueless." You say, "She has a refreshingly original approach to reality." Politeness becomes your blade. This works because the delivery feels objective, like you're reviewing a meal, rather than cutting down a person. It also forces the listener to decipher the insult, which adds a layer of sophistication. By the time they realise they've been insulted, the conversation has already moved on to the next topic. Well done, you!

4. **Value over volume.** This is really the golden rule of all intelligent humour. It means that one well-timed, well-crafted insult will land better than a string of poorly-chosen, obvious ones. Anyone can hurl a dozen mediocre jabs, but what sets the British apart is their ability to deliver a single line that stops people in their tracks. It's about saying the most...while also saying the least. Think of simple lines like, "Well, that was a choice." Brief, but gets the point across louder than yelling a hundred profanities. So, when you're crafting an insult, ask yourself: Does this say something, or am I just speaking for the sake of it? If it's forgettable, it's noise.

Now that you understand the basics, join me as we tour the insults. Page by page, I'll guide you through the meaning, the madness, and of course, real-world examples. Rest assured, once you know them, you'll never lose another passive-aggressive battle again. Let's crack on, shall we?

Classic British Insults

Designed for the everyday moments, from a night out at the pub to the queue at Tesco.

NAFF

Definition: Something uncool, tacky, or generally unfashionable.

At a party:

That jacket is absolutely naff. Who let him wear that?

At work:

This presentation looks a bit naff; we'll need to jazz it up.

At the pub:

You're wearing naff trainers to the pub? Bold choice, mate.

In conversation:

Her attitude was naff, like she couldn't be bothered.

With mates:

You've bought the naffest Christmas jumper I've ever seen.

DODGY

Definition: Suspicious, untrustworthy, or questionable in quality or behaviour.

At the pub:

That pint tastes a bit dodgy—are you sure the keg hasn't gone off?

On the street:

I wouldn't trust that dodgy bloke trying to sell phones out of a van.

At work:

The figures in this report look dodgy; someone's been fiddling the numbers.

With mates:

This kebab van looks a bit dodgy. Let's hope we don't regret it tomorrow!

NUMPTY

Definition: A lovable fool, someone who is clumsy or makes silly mistakes.

At the pub:

Don't be a numpty, your pint's spilling everywhere!

At work:

That numpty sent the email to the entire company instead of just me.

At home:

You numpty! You've put the dishwasher tablets in the washing machine!

With mates:

He's such a numpty for locking himself out twice in one day.

In traffic:

Look at that numpty driving with his boot wide open.

PLONKER

Definition: A fool, often used affectionately for someone being a bit silly.

At the pub:

You're a plonker for ordering a cocktail in a beer garden.

At work:

The plonker printed the report upside down!

With mates:

You absolute plonker, you've forgotten your wallet again!

At home:

Mum's being a bit of a plonker, thinking she can rewire the lights herself.

At a football match:

Our striker's a plonker, he's missed an open goal!

MUPPET

Definition: Someone acting daft, often in a harmless or comedic way.

At work:

You're such a muppet for hitting "reply all" by accident.

With mates:

You muppet, you've booked us a table at the wrong restaurant!

At the pub:

He's acting like a muppet, trying to win a trivia game he knows nothing about.

On the street:

Look at that muppet parking diagonally across two spaces.

At home:

Stop being a muppet and help me carry these groceries!

WALLY

Definition: A silly or inept person, often harmlessly clueless.

At the pub:

Look at that wally spilling his pint down his shirt.

At work:

Who's the wally that sent the email to the wrong department?

With mates:

You wally, that's not your phone—it's the TV remote!

At home:

Mum's being a bit of a wally, forgetting where she parked the car again.

In traffic:

That wally's driving with the handbrake on.

PILLOCK

Definition: A fool or idiot, often behaving in a particularly clumsy or stupid way.

At the pub:

That pillock just knocked over three pints in one go.

At work:

Only a pillock would schedule a meeting at 5:00 p.m. on a Friday.

With mates:

You're a pillock for thinking you could eat an entire curry on your own.

At home:

Dad's being a pillock, trying to fix the sink without turning off the water first.

At a football match:

Our goalie's a pillock for letting that ball slip through his hands!

BERK

Definition: A fool, derived from Cockney rhyming slang (Berkshire Hunt). A mildly insulting but not vulgar term.

At the pub:

Don't be such a berk, just order a proper pint.

At work:

He's a berk for forgetting to save his work before the computer crashed.

With mates:

Stop acting like a berk and help me carry this sofa.

At a party:

That berk just spilled red wine on the new carpet!

In traffic:

What a berk, he's been indicating left for the past mile.

WAZZOCK

Definition: A completely useless or foolish individual.

At the pub:

That wazzock just knocked over three chairs trying to sit down.

At work:

The wazzock emailed the entire company instead of just their team.

With mates:

Don't be a wazzock, stop trying to park in a space that's too small.

At home:

Dad's being a wazzock, thinking he can fix the sink without turning the water off.

In traffic:

Some wazzock cut across three lanes without signalling.

BLAGGER

Definition: Someone who pretends to know more than they do.

At the pub:

He's such a blagger, claiming to know all the answers to the quiz.

At work:

That blagger just took credit for the team's entire project.

With mates:

You're a blagger if you think you can win without even practising.

At home:

Stop being a blagger, you've never fixed anything in your life!

In traffic:

That blagger pretended to have a flat just to get ahead in the queue.

PRAT

Definition: A mildly insulting term for an annoying or stupid individual.

At the pub:

That prat spilled half his pint trying to show off his dance moves.

At work:

The prat forgot to unmute himself during the entire meeting.

With mates:

You're such a prat for thinking you could outrun the bus.

At home:

Mum's being a prat, trying to carry six bags of shopping at once.

In traffic:

Look at that prat tailgating everyone on the motorway.

PLANK

Definition: Someone particularly dense or lacking common sense.

At the pub:

He's a total plank for ordering wine at a beer festival.

At work:

That plank printed the report upside down and backwards.

With mates:

You plank, why would you try to barbecue indoors?

At home:

Dad's being a plank, thinking the Wi-Fi will fix itself if he just stares at it.

In traffic:

Some plank parked across two spaces in the car park.

PILL

Definition: An irritating or tiresome person.

At the pub:

Don't be such a pill, just order something already.

At work:

He's a pill for always turning up late and leaving early.

With mates:

You're a pill for bringing a board game nobody wanted to play.

At home:

Mum's being a pill, insisting we redecorate the living room again.

In traffic:

That pill's been hooting for five minutes straight.

PONCE

Definition: Someone pretentious or affected, often overly concerned with appearance.

At the pub:

Look at that ponce, asking if the beer is organic.

At work:

The ponce just sent another email full of flowery language that says nothing.

With mates:

Stop being a ponce and eat the burger, it's not meant to be fancy.

At home:

Dad's such a ponce about his garden, refusing to let anyone walk on the grass.

In traffic:

That ponce is polishing their car while parked in the loading zone.

DULLARD

Definition: A slow-witted or uninteresting person.

At the pub:

That dullard's been telling the same story for an hour.

At work:

The dullard in accounting keeps explaining spreadsheets no one asked about.

With mates:

You dullard, why would you wear flip-flops to a hiking trail?

At home:

Mum's being a dullard, watching the same soap opera reruns all weekend.

In traffic:

Some dullard is blocking the exit because they're checking their phone.

BELLEND

Definition: An idiot or jerk.

At work:

Gavin unplugged my laptop to charge his vape. Absolute bellend.

At the pub:

He ordered a rosé and started quoting Nietzsche. What a bellend.

In traffic:

Cut me off, then had the nerve to wave. Bellend behaviour.

At the shops:

Argued with a cashier over a 5p bag. Proper bellend.

At home:

Left his boxers on the kitchen chair again. Bellend.

SOD

Definition: Someone annoying, lazy, or unfortunate.

At work:

He's off sick again? Lucky sod.

At the pub:

Her boyfriend forgot her birthday. What a sod.

In traffic:

That poor sod's been waiting to merge for a decade.

At the shops:

Look at that sod trying to scan ten avocados on self-checkout.

On holiday:

It rained all week. Typical sods, us.

TOSSPOT

Definition: An annoying or ridiculous person. Usually said about someone acting foolish or self-important.

At work:

He called a "stand-up" just to read his own email out loud. Tosspot.

At the pub:

He's had two pints and now he's doing impressions. Tosspot alert.

In traffic:

Nice indicator, tosspot. Ever heard of it?

At the gym:

Wearing fingerless gloves like it's 2004. Tosspot.

On Zoom:

He unmuted just to sigh loudly. What a tosspot.

MINGER

Definition: Someone unattractive.

At work:

Someone microwaved fish again. The whole office smells like a minger's sock.

At the pub:

Tried to flirt with me. Breath like bin juice. Full-on minger.

On public transport:

Took his shoes off on the train. Actual minger.

At the shops:

Picking her nose in the cereal aisle. Minging behaviour.

At home:

I've been in the same hoodie for three days. Feel like a right minger.

NINNY

Definition: Fool or simpleton. Used endearingly.

At work:

He printed the entire presentation upside down. Ninny.

At the pub:

Peter spilled his pint before the toast. Classic ninny.

In traffic:

He tried to reverse and hit a bollard. What a ninny.

At the shops:

Left her handbag in the trolley. Poor ninny.

With family:

Mum used salt instead of sugar again. Sweet old ninny.

CODGER

Definition: An elderly, grumpy, or eccentric man. Usually used as "old codger."

At work:

The IT guy still uses a flip phone. Proper old codger.

At the pub:

Some codger's been sat in my seat since three.

In traffic:

That codger's doing twenty in a forty and swerving all over the place.

At the shops:

Argued over the price of corned beef. Codger move.

At home:

My dad still prints out his emails. Love the old codger.

Posh & Aristocratic Insults

These insults are perfect for the refined among us: cutting but elegant, with just a touch of haughty disdain.

CAD

Definition: A man of low morals, often a shameless flirt or manipulator.

At a party:

He's such a cad, flirting with every woman here!

With mates:

Stop being a cad and give her some space, mate.

At work:

That cad tried to take credit for my idea in the meeting.

At a family gathering:

Uncle George is a proper cad, always regifting presents.

At the pub:

What a cad, sneaking off without paying for his round!

BOUNDER

Definition: An ill-mannered, unsophisticated person who oversteps social boundaries.

At a restaurant:

What a bounder, eating before everyone else has been served!

In conversation:

He's a bounder for interrupting the host repeatedly.

At the pub:

The bounder didn't even say thanks after we bought him a drink.

At work:

That bounder tried to steal someone else's desk!

At a wedding:

The bounder showed up in jeans, how disgraceful!

CHURLISH

Definition: Rude or mean-spirited behaviour, often lacking manners or gratitude.

At work:

It's churlish not to thank someone for helping you.

At a party:

Don't be churlish, at least try to enjoy yourself.

With mates:

That was churlish of you, not sharing your crisps.

At a family dinner:

It's churlish not to offer tea to your guests.

At the pub:

He's being churlish, complaining about everything without offering a solution.

POMPOUS TWIT

Definition: A self-important, often clueless person who loves to brag.

At work:

Our manager's a pompous twit, always quoting himself in emails.

At the pub:

That bloke's a pompous twit, lecturing everyone about craft beers.

With mates:

Stop being a pompous twit, it's just a game of darts!

At a restaurant:

That pompous twit keeps name-dropping celebrities.

At a football match:

He's such a pompous twit, acting like he's the coach.

CHEEKY BEGGAR

Definition: Someone audacious or shameless in a humorous way.

At work:

The cheeky beggar asked for a raise after being late all week!

At the pub:

You cheeky beggar, trying to pinch my chips.

With mates:

He's a cheeky beggar, always talking his way into VIP areas.

At a family gathering:

You cheeky beggar, taking the biggest slice of cake!

On the street:

That cheeky beggar tried to sell me a watch while wearing two!

SWINE

Definition: A rude, greedy, ill-mannered person.

At work:

Left me out of the lunch order again, the swine.

At the pub:

Nicked the last sausage roll. Absolute swine.

In traffic:

Cut me off and didn't indicate. Swine behind the wheel.

At the shops:

Charged me for two loaves. The swine thought I wouldn't notice.

At home:

Ate my leftovers and blamed the cat. Swine move.

RAKE

Definition: A man who participates in immoral behaviour, particularly a womanizer.

At work:

Flirts with everyone in marketing. Bit of a rake, that one.

At the pub:

Three pints in and he's quoting Byron. God, he's a rake.

In traffic:

Convertible. Elbow out. Classic rake energy.

At the shops:

He winked at the cashier. Full rake mode.

At a party:

Turned up in velvet. Red wine in hand. He's a rake and he knows it.

BLIGHTER

Definition: A scoundrel or rascal.

At work:

Spilled coffee on the report again. Clumsy blighter.

At the pub:

He's bought everyone a round except me. Cheeky blighter.

In traffic:

That blighter's parked sideways. Brilliant.

At the shops:

Grabbed the last pack of crumpets. Lucky little blighter.

At home:

The boiler's gone again. Bloody blighter of a thing.

MISCREANT

Definition: A rule-breaker.

At work:

Who deleted the shared file? Identify the miscreant.

At the pub:

Miscreant stole my pint while I was in the loo.

In traffic:

That miscreant's texting while driving. Unbelievable.

At the shops:

Some miscreants swapped the price tags. Thought they were clever.

At home (about kids/pets):

Found the biscuits under the sofa. Which miscreant was responsible?

PHILISTINE

Definition: Someone with no taste, culture, or appreciation for art or intellect.

At work:

He called Shakespeare "a bit long." Utter philistine.

At the pub:

Wouldn't try the Stilton. Says cheese shouldn't smell. What a philistine.

In traffic:

Listening to autotuned nonsense at full blast. Philistine on wheels.

At the shops:

Bought instant coffee over fresh grounds. Philistine behaviour.

At home:

Said my mid-century chairs looked "old." Can't argue with a philistine.

PLEB

Definition: Someone uncouth or uncultured. Short for "plebeian."

At work:

He microwaved fish in an open office. Complete pleb.

At the pub:

He ordered a lager top and asked for ketchup. Pleb alert.

In traffic:

Revving his engine like a pleb in a boy racer car.

At the shops:

Arguing about a loyalty card for 20p. Utter pleb.

At home:

My flat mate used my best knife to open Amazon boxes. I live with a pleb.

PART 2

The Art of the British Backhanded Compliment

A British compliment is very rarely just a compliment. It can sound polite, but if you listen very closely, there's usually something else hidden beneath. A small dig, or a small twist of the knife. It's delivered with a smile, sometimes a smirk, and often followed by an awkward silence. If you're new to the culture, you might actually take it at face value. Locals know better.

This section is all about one of Britain's most notable social skills: the backhanded compliment. It's not an insult, not quite. We Brits walk the line: just charming enough to disarm, just cutting enough to remind you who's winning. It's not about being nasty. It's about being clever without ever raising your voice.

Direct praise, much like direct insults, can feel a bit too much here. It's too open, too earnest. So instead, we tone it down. We say things like, "You've done well for yourself."

Translation: We're shocked you've made it this far, or "You're quite bold to do that." Translation: Questionable choice, but points for confidence. These remarks aren't always meant to sting; in fact, sometimes they're a form of affection. The more backhanded the compliment, the more likely it came from someone who secretly admires the recipient. It can be used as a way to undermine their social power, or subtly assert your own, without ever breaking the rules of civility. If you can use it well, you understand the rhythm of British life. If you can recognise it when it's used on you, you'll save yourself some embarrassment. And if you can master it? Congratulations! You're officially British.

So, what actually is a backhanded compliment? And how is it different from plain old sarcasm? At its core, the British backhanded compliment follows a very specific formula: a bit of praise, immediately negated by something that takes the shine off. It's a compliment with a twist. Just sharp enough to make you pause and wonder: Was that nice...or not? It's not as blunt as sarcasm, which usually signals itself with tone. And it's not as mean-spirited as a full-on direct insult, which is designed to undermine confidence. The British version is more elegant. It's subtle. You're meant to smile, accept it graciously, and only later, perhaps while brushing your teeth or lying in bed, realise what was actually said.

Take this, for example: "I like your confidence." That's genuine. "You're very brave to wear those trousers." That's not. That's classic British, and brutal. The genius of it lies in the delivery: warm tone, maybe a smile, and not a hint of malice...on the surface. You'll know a backhanded compliment when you hear one, though you may miss it at first. Sometimes it takes a few seconds (or hours) to sink in.

A few classics you'll likely encounter: "You look well! I didn't recognise you." Translation: You usually look terrible, but I'll hold my tongue. "I wish I had the confidence to dance like that." Translation: I would never do that, but you do you. "You're smarter than you let on." Translation: You've certainly been fooling us all this time. "You've done so well for yourself." Translation: Who would've thought? "You've lost weight, are you okay?" Translation: You definitely look better, but also possibly ill.

It's an art form. Delivered with the right tone, these can pass as genuine kindness. Delivered poorly, they become social disasters. They're not blurted out at random, they're strategic.

Here's where they tend to appear:

- **Dinner parties:** Just formal enough to keep things civil, just casual enough for a little mischief.
- **Workplaces:** Especially during performance reviews, office birthdays, or when someone's leaving.
- **Family gatherings:** Often delivered by an aunt or uncle who (sort of) means well.
- **Pubs:** After two drinks, subtlety disappears. The compliments get bolder, the hits get stronger.

This isn't just pettiness, it's cultural. Brits are famously indirect. A blunt statement feels too raw. It makes people uncomfortable. It implies sincerity, emotion, vulnerability, and potential retaliation. Risky business. A backhanded compliment allows someone to level the playing field without ever seeming impolite. It's emotional warfare with a smile, and there's a formula to doing it right. Follow it, and you'll sound charming. Get it wrong, and you'll sound mean. Keep your tone light and slightly amused, never sharp. Maintain a neutral or pleasant expression. No smirking. Use words like "brave," "interesting," or "bold," and leave just enough of a pause. For example: "That's...an impressive choice."

And most importantly: Stop talking once you've let it out. Don't explain. The more you explain, the less British it becomes. The key is standing by what you've just said, and not letting the potential response rattle you. Should you find yourself on the receiving end of a backhanded compliment, don't get defensive. Respond in kind: drily and with a dash of humour.

Some golden go-to replies:

"Thank you...I think?"

"I'll take that as a compliment."

Or simply raise an eyebrow, offer a tight smile, and move the conversation along.

Backhanded Compliments vs. Outright Insults

There is a line. A good backhanded compliment is sly. It toes the line, but never quite crosses it. If the tone is too harsh or the delivery too obvious, it stops being clever and becomes just rude. A poorly executed snub leaves no room for ambiguity, and therefore, no room for escape. If you've overstepped? Retreat with grace. Laugh it off. Blame the wine. Change the subject.

It's not about cruelty, it's about control. Backhanded compliments aren't there to wound. They're there to reestablish hierarchy. To signal, softly, where everyone stands. Once you can wield them well, you've passed a sort of test. You're fluent in a very specific, very British type of humour, hierarchy, and human behaviour.

Next challenge? Knowing when to say nothing at all. Because, in Britain, silence is sometimes the most powerful message. Here, silence isn't empty, it's loaded with implication. It says, "I heard that and I'm choosing not to dignify it." In other words, tread carefully. Silence allows a window of time for the perpetrator to think about (read: fear) what happens next. It gives them space to marinate in their own words, which segues into what is perhaps the most powerful aspect overall: silence makes the other person uncomfortable, not you. Imagine: You're sipping your tea and they're sat there wondering, "Have I overstepped?" "Did I cross a line?" Using silence elegantly is not about a lack of words. It's the choice not to lower yourself to using them.

Which brings me to my next topic: British facial expressions. These are their own dialect of insult. There is an entire catalogue of nonverbal retorts that can shame, dismiss, or entirely annihilate someone—all without a single word spoken. Let's walk through some of them, shall we?

The tight-lipped smile
Translation: You're embarrassing yourself and I'm going to give you one last chance to stop.

The single eyebrow raise
Translation: Really? *Really?*

The long blink and head tilt
Translation: I know you didn't just say that.

The nose breath chuckle
Translation: You're an absolute joke, but I won't say so... with words.

The sharp inhale through the teeth
Translation: Oh no...can't stop you now.

The goldfish blink then look away
Translation: I won't even bother responding to that.

The fixed smile with dead eyes
Translation: I despise you and I'm fantasizing about your downfall as you speak.

Most terrifying of all? The total freeze-out. If someone really (and I mean really) hates you, they won't dignify you with an expression at all. They'll just stare at you blankly, as if to signal to you that you are so irrelevant...you may as well not exist at all.

Full-On Phrases

Bold, unapologetic expressions that deliver the perfect punch with maximum British flair.

YOU'RE HAVING A LAUGH

Definition: A sarcastic way of saying something is ridiculous.

At work:

You're having a laugh if you think I'm staying late on a Friday.

At the pub:

Five quid for a pint? You're having a laugh!

With mates:

You're having a laugh if you think I'm running a marathon with you.

In traffic:

You're having a laugh if you think I'm letting you cut in.

At home:

You're having a laugh if you think I'm doing the washing-up tonight.

LOST THE PLOT

Definition: Acting irrationally or out of control.

At work:

The boss has lost the plot, scheduling meetings at 7:00 a.m.

At the pub:

He's lost the plot if he thinks he can drink five pints in an hour.

With mates:

You've lost the plot, mate. That idea's ridiculous.

At a family dinner:

Mum's lost the plot, redecorating the house for the third time this year.

In traffic:

That driver's lost the plot, weaving all over the road.

TAKING THE PISS

Definition: To mock or make fun of someone.

At work:

They're taking the piss if they think I'll work overtime for free.

At the pub:

Stop taking the piss and tell me what you really think.

With mates:

He's always taking the piss out of my cooking.

At home:

You're taking the piss, asking me to clean your room too!

On the street:

That guy's taking the piss, charging twenty quid for a fake watch.

AS USEFUL AS A CHOCOLATE TEAPOT

Definition: Completely useless or ineffective.

At work:

This report is as useful as a chocolate teapot, nothing makes sense.

At the pub:

The Wi-Fi here is as useful as a chocolate teapot.

With mates:

You're as useful as a chocolate teapot when it comes to directions.

At home:

This tin opener is as useful as a chocolate teapot, it doesn't work!

At a football match:

The ref's as useful as a chocolate teapot, missing every foul.

NOT THE SHARPEST TOOL IN THE BOX

Definition: A polite way of saying someone isn't very smart.

At work:

He's not the sharpest tool in the box, but he means well.

With mates:

Bless her, she's not the sharpest tool in the box, but she tries her best.

At the pub:

The bloke behind the bar's not the sharpest tool in the box, is he?

At home:

Stop acting like you're not the sharpest tool in the box and read the manual.

In traffic:

That driver's not the sharpest tool in the box, he keeps missing the exits.

DON'T BE DAFT

Definition: Don't be ridiculous.

At home:

You're going to fix the boiler yourself? Don't be daft, you nearly electrocuted yourself changing a lightbulb.

At work:

You think the boss actually likes those 8:00 a.m. meetings? Don't be daft. He's just punishing us.

In class:

You think she revised for this? Don't be daft, she's been on TikTok all week.

At the gym:

Don't be daft, of course I'm not doing leg day two days in a row.

With mates:

He said he'd marry you if West Ham won the league? Don't be daft, that's never happening.

PULL THE OTHER ONE, IT'S GOT BELLS ON

Definition: A phrase signalling disbelief.

At home:

You made the bed? Pull the other one, it's got bells on, I saw the duvet still in a heap.

At work:

He reckons he hit Q2 targets in his sleep? Pull the other one.

In class:

Oh sure, your dog ate your coursework and logged into Turnitin. Pull the other one.

At the gym:

You benched 225 after three weeks off? Pull the other one, mate.

With mates:

She said she's never touched Botox. Pull the other one, her forehead hasn't moved since Easter.

LOAD OF TOSH

Definition: A load of nonsense.

At home:

He says he "forgot" to take the bin out again. What a load of tosh.

At work:

The new policy says it'll "empower team synergy." Absolute tosh.

In class:

This article claims Napoleon was misunderstood. Tosh. He was 5'6" and angry.

At the gym:

He's on TikTok saying pre-workout supplements cured his anxiety. Load of tosh.

With mates:

She reckons horoscopes predicted her ex cheating? Tosh. That was just Tinder and bad decisions.

THICK AS TWO SHORT PLANKS

Definition: Someone stupid and silly.

At home:

He put the frozen pizza in the oven with the plastic still on. Thick as two short planks.

At work:

She cc'd the entire company instead of just HR. Two short planks, honestly.

In class:

He asked if Shakespeare was still alive. Thick as two short planks.

At the gym:

He thought "deadlift" meant you had to lie down first.

With mates:

She tried to microwave a metal bowl. Bless her, thick as two short planks.

GOT A (BIT OF A) SCREW LOOSE

Definition: Not quite all there, behaving erratically or strangely.

At home:

Mum's reorganised the cupboard by food colour. She's got a bit of a screw loose.

At work:

He just volunteered to do another shift. Screw loose, that one.

In class:

She submitted a twenty-eight-page essay for a five-hundred-word brief. Got a screw loose.

At the gym:

He's doing burpees for fun. Screw loose, obviously.

With mates:

She invited her ex to her birthday. I'm telling you, there's a screw loose there.

COULDN'T ORGANISE A PISS-UP IN A BREWERY

Definition: Utterly useless at planning.

At home:

She tried to plan Christmas dinner and forgot the turkey. Couldn't organise a piss-up in a brewery.

At work:

We had four managers and still no projector. Honestly, couldn't organise a piss-up.

In class:

The group project leader couldn't organise a piss-up in a brewery. He missed the deadline...and the topic.

At the gym:

He booked a personal training session and forgot to show up. He couldn't organise a piss-up in a brewery, that one.

With mates:

He planned a pub crawl and didn't check opening hours. We ended up at Greggs. Couldn't organise a piss-up, honestly.

MORE NERVE THAN SENSE

Definition: Bold, but foolish.

At home:

She told Auntie Jean she doesn't like her cooking. More nerve than sense.

At work:

He tried to negotiate a raise the day after missing a deadline. Nerve, but no sense.

In class:

She's got more nerve than sense. She turned in a blank paper and argued for an A on "energy" alone.

At the gym:

Tried to outlift the trainer. Herniated a disc. More nerve than sense.

With mates:

She flirted with his girlfriend right in front of him. More nerve than sense, that one.

Situational Insults

For the most quotidian of moments. Keep these in your repertoire, and you'll always be prepared.

For Driving

Use these when you're out on the road. For safety, mutter these under your breath and don't actually shout them to passersby.

- Indicating is free, love. Treat yourself.
- If you drove any slower, you'd be reversing time.
- Your licence came in a cereal box, didn't it?
- I've seen more spatial awareness in a teaspoon.
- You brake like you're being paid by the stop.

For the Pub

Use these for a night out with your mates.

- One more pint and you'll finally have a personality.
- Didn't realise they let toddlers drink pints now.
- You drink like it's a talent. It isn't.
- That joke was aged in the cellar with the ale.
- I'd toast to your wit, but it never turned up.

For Work

Use when justified...and willing to be let go.

- I'd ask for your input, but I need results.
- You bring a lot to the table, mainly dead weight.
- Micromanaging is not a skill, it's a cry for help.
- Every meeting with you is a TED Talk with no point.
- That idea's so bad it needs a trigger warning.

- Your emails are a desperate cry for a sabbatical.
- I'd say "good job," but I value honesty.
- You speak fluent corporate buzzword and zero sense.

For Family Gatherings

Use these when holidays with your extended family become a bit too much.

- Ah, the annual reminder that genetics are a dice roll.
- Imagine being the cautionary tale at your own reunion.
- You've really leaned into being the disappointing one.

For a Night Out

For a wild Friday night with your best mates.

- You're one cocktail from making poor life choices...again.
- Dancing like the floor's on fire doesn't count as rhythm.
- Your flirting has the finesse of a fire alarm.

For the Football Match

Use these to defend your club's honour.

- Even the ref's guide dog is embarrassed.
- Your team defends like it's optional.
- If passion won trophies, you'd still be empty-handed.
- I've seen tighter formations in toddlers' finger painting.

For the Tube

For your delightful morning and afternoon commute.

- That perfume is bloody criminal.
- Standing that close should come with dinner first.
- Yes, shove in. We're all here for the group sauna.
- You look like you've never seen a queue or a mirror.
- Mind the gap between your manners and reality.

For the Neighbour

Use when struggling to tolerate the people who live next door.

- He mows the grass like it's offended him.
- Your DIY's more "try" than "do."
- That wind chime's about as musical as a car alarm.
- Your welcome mat's lying.

For the Queue Jumper

Frankly, it's criminal. They deserve the lot.

- There he is, the main character of Tesco.
- Oh, by all means, your time is obviously more important.
- You must have mistaken this for a race. It isn't.
- The back of the queue is just behind your entitlement.
- If I wanted to be ignored, I'd call my ex.

For the Online Comments Section

If you must respond, respond with grace...and let it draw blood.

- Bold of you to be this loud and this wrong.
- Your keyboard should file for abuse.
- You've mistaken Google for a degree again.
- Your opinion is noted. By absolutely no one.

For the In-Laws

Refrain from using these if you enjoy being married and want to stay that way.

- Every time you speak, I hear the wedding bells fade.
- Thanks for dinner. Next time, I'll bring earplugs.
- Your parenting advice is almost as outdated as your decor.

PART 3

Historical Insults from British Figures

Allow me to take you back in time. Throughout the ages, insults have been a tool of communication. I'd wager even the cavemen were etching cutting remarks into stone—probably about someone's fire-starting technique. While the vast majority of these put-downs have gone undocumented, we are fortunate that many have survived. As the £2 coin says, "We are all standing on the shoulders of giants," and in this case, those giants were cruelly articulate. They walked, so you and I could run. This part is for them. Here are some of my absolute favourite historical blows, and a reminder that wit ages far better than civility.

Winston Churchill to Lady Astor:

Lady Astor: "If I were your wife, I'd poison your tea."
Winston Churchill: "If I were your husband, I'd drink it."

Documented in multiple Churchill biographies and history texts, this anecdote is elite-tier British wordplay—petty, polished, and served with wine. Nancy Astor was the first female member of Parliament, and she loathed Winston Churchill. Judging by his quick retort and clear disdain for her existence, the feeling was quite mutual. This exchange became the stuff of legends.

Samuel Johnson on a rival's manuscript:

"Sir, your manuscript is both good and original. But the part that is good is not original; and the part that is original is not good."

Samuel Johnson was a writer, poet, playwright, essayist, and evidently, not one to mince words or show restraint. Whether he disliked this particular rival or simply loathed mediocrity, the line slices through both flattery and originality like the guillotine. It's a textbook eighteenth-century takedown: refined, brutal, and under twenty words.

Winston Churchill on Clement Attlee:

"An empty taxi arrived, and when the door was opened, Attlee got out."

Said after a public event at 10 Downing Street, this jab was aimed squarely at Clement Attlee, Churchill's successor, political opposite, and apparently a human beige cardigan. Their relationship was famously frosty, and Churchill rarely missed a chance to mock Attlee's dullness. This line? A master class in minimum words, maximum damage.

Oscar Wilde:

“Some cause happiness wherever they go; others, whenever they go.”

You’ll find this in every Wilde collection worth its salt, and for good reason. Whether aimed at overstaying guests or a dinner party attendee devoid of personality, it’s a reminder that Wilde didn’t just insult people. He eviscerated them. Elegantly.

Insult like a Lady or Gentleman

A quick guide on delivering insults with grace and charm. Perfect for upscale social gatherings or more formal settings.

To insult like a lady or gentleman, you must master the art of socially acceptable brutality. The kind that cuts deep without ever shouting or tarnishing your reputation. It's not about profanity, and it's not about raising your voice. It's about letting your opinion be known, discreetly, and never leaving room for your victim to lose the plot entirely. Here's how it's done:

1. **Ask questions that are actually statements.** Passive aggression, polished. "You must be exhausted keeping up that level of confidence, no?" Or, "Did you mean to say that out loud?" Translation: We all know you meant to say that out loud, but it's so much more amusing to make you stew in it, isn't it?
2. **Master the backhanded compliment.** Make it sound like praise, then let them wonder. Revisit Part 2 to truly understand this.
3. **Use impeccable manners as camouflage.** The more polite the phrasing, the sharper the knife. Perfect example: "Forgive me, I thought you were joking." Bravo! A truly elegant and sophisticated insult leaves the audience not just scratching their heads until realisation sets in, but admiring your perfect form.

Let's review a few different types of refined insults, befitting a duke or duchess.

Polite Disdain

- Oh, how quaint of you to still believe that.
- It's remarkable how you always manage to find the least efficient way.

Subtle Critique

- That's an interesting interpretation. Bold, even.
- I do admire your confidence in that opinion.

Playful Sarcasm

- Oh, I didn't realise we were exchanging opinions, but do continue.
- How charmingly naïve of you.

Highbrow Comebacks

- A bold critique, though perhaps next time try one with substance.
- You must be quite the expert, though I hadn't noticed before.

Insults for the Clueless

A selection of witty jabs to be used when the lights are on but nobody is home.

BLITHERING IDIOT

Definition: A completely clueless or foolish person, often babbling nonsense.

At work:

The blithering idiot forgot to attach the file to the email.

With mates:

Don't be a blithering idiot, just read the instructions!

At the pub:

That blithering idiot spilled his drink and blamed the bartender.

In traffic:

Look at that blithering idiot, stopping in the middle of the road!

At a restaurant:

The blithering idiot tried to serve champagne with fish.

GORMLESS

Definition: Lacking intelligence or common sense, often appearing clueless.

At work:

He's gormless for not realising the deadline was yesterday.

With mates:

Stop looking so gormless and just answer the question!

At the pub:

You look gormless standing there, what'll you have to drink?

At home:

You're gormless for putting the milk in the cupboard again.

In traffic:

That gormless driver just ran a red light.

NINCOMPOOP

Definition: A foolish or incompetent person, used humorously.

At work:

You nincompoop, you've deleted the wrong file again!

With mates:

You're such a nincompoop, thinking you can climb that wall.

At the pub:

That nincompoop just spilled his pint all over the table.

At home:

Stop acting like a nincompoop and follow the recipe properly.

In traffic:

What a nincompoop, he's driving on the wrong side of the road!

DAFT AS A BRUSH

Definition: Someone very silly or lacking common sense.

At work:

She's daft as a brush, trying to photocopy her phone screen.

With mates:

Don't be daft as a brush, we can't swim in this weather!

At home:

He's daft as a brush, thinking the oven preheats in thirty seconds.

At the pub:

You're daft as a brush if you think you can drink six pints and cycle home.

In traffic:

That driver's daft as a brush, reversing into oncoming traffic.

SPANNER

Definition: A clumsy, foolish person who makes a mess of things.

At work:

Who's the total spanner that locked us out of the office?

At the pub:

He's a total spanner, knocking over all the chairs while trying to sit down.

With mates:

Don't be a total spanner, you know you can't win at darts.

At home:

Mum's being a total spanner, putting the washing machine on without any detergent.

In traffic:

Look at that total spanner parking in two spaces.

PART 4

The Insult Comeback Guide

Picture it: You're at the pub having a pint, mate mid-sentence, when suddenly...someone insults you. Right to your face. You're stunned, you're flabbergasted, but...you're British. So, what do you do? You send a comeback their way that is so devastating, they may never speak again. Much like an insult, a comeback is never about yelling. This section isn't about starting fights; it's about finishing them. With class. Read on carefully, as I'm going to teach you three important lessons. If used wisely, the next time you're insulted, you'll be fully prepared to respond with humour, wit, and lethal charm.

Lesson 1: Know Thy Opponent

A good comeback is tailor-made for the occasion. You want them to understand that you are, in fact, clapping back. It should have an air of "I see your insult, and I raise you a far more eloquent and intelligent one." In order to do this effectively, you need to understand a few things: Was their insult made in jest, or a serious offense? Where were you?

Can this person even handle your response? Clock it all before you speak.

Lesson 2: The Comeback Formula

There are three crucial components to a retort that leaves a mark. First, timing. Wait a beat. Let them marinate, and fear what's coming next. Second, tone is everything. Stay dry, stay calm, and remain completely unbothered. Nothing ruins a comeback like letting the enemy know they've gotten under your skin. Imagine a school bully: He steals your lunch, and you cry on the playground. Bully: 1. You: 0. This is no different. Third, weaponise your wit. You don't want to beat them at their own game; you want to play at a new level entirely. The real triumph in delivering the perfect comeback is less about what you say to them, and more about making it abundantly clear that their jabs could never be as sophisticated or intelligent as yours. It's social superiority. The moment you react like their insult is beneath your retaliation, they're beneath you...end of. Your comeback isn't to defend yourself; it's to reveal their shortcomings. It silently implies, "We're not the same. You'd need a map, a ladder, and a prayer to reach my level." No yelling, no vulgarity, just razor-like wit.

Lesson 3: Ready, Aim, Fire

Your goal? Pure logic, zero emotion. Example: Someone says to you, "Still drinking that shandy? You never really grew up, did you?" Others may balk and flail at this comment, but not you. You hit them with, "Imagine needing stronger alcohol just to feel interesting." Then you take a sip of your shandy, turn away, and rejoin your mates. Bullseye.

This wouldn't be *The Definitive Guide to British Insults* without putting an arsenal of comebacks at your disposal. These are categorized for any and all scenarios. Keep these in your back pocket and be ready to fire at a moment's notice. Aim with caution!

When They Call You Dumb

- Ah. Still going with confidence over accuracy, I see.
- Brave, coming from someone who lost to Google Docs.
- It must be exhausting, mistakenly thinking you're clever all day.
- Honestly, the stupidest thing I've done all day is endure your presence.

When They Call You Ugly

- I don't take fashion tips from people who dress like stress personified.
- You'd know...you've been staring.
- That's rich, coming from a face only a mother could love.
- I've been called worse by better people.
- Wait, you can see? And you still chose to leave the house like that? Bold.
- Ugly can be fixed, stupid can't.

When They Call You Boring, Weak, or Irrelevant

- You talk like your opinion means something to me.
- Sorry, who are you again?
- It's sweet that you think I need your validation.
- Oh, it's you. I forgot you existed.
- Thank you for your unsolicited and irrelevant opinion.

Polite British Claps (for Workplaces or In-Laws)

- Mm. Brave of you to share that out loud.
- Did you mean to say that, or did it accidentally escape?
- Gosh. Imagine having to explain that to your therapist.
- I don't have the time or the crayons to explain this to you.

Modern British Insults

Savage one-liners and cutting comebacks for the twenty-first century Brit who insults with style.

DIMWIT

Definition: A stupid or silly person.

At work:

The dimwit in accounts just emailed the entire company instead of the client.

At the pub:

Only a dimwit orders a pint of Foster's in a proper boozer.

At a football match:

Some dimwit showed up in the wrong team's colours. Brave or brainless, hard to tell.

At a restaurant:

He asked if the bangers were vegetarian. Dimwit.

At home:

Mum, your precious son just tried microwaving foil. Again. Absolute dimwit.

HALFWIT

Definition: Someone unintelligent. See: "Dimwit."

At work:

He copied the boss into an email slagging off the boss. Certified halfwit.

At the pub:

You don't tell your ex's new bloke you still miss her, you halfwit.

At a football match:

Only a halfwit leaves ten minutes early "to beat the traffic" when we're 1–1 in stoppage time.

At a restaurant:

He sent back the steak because it was pink. What a halfwit.

At home:

I live with a halfwit who thinks the Wi-Fi resets faster if you shout at it.

CLUELESS WONDER

Definition: Someone who has not a clue, yet somehow still makes their way.

At work:

Clueless wonder asked what GDPR is. He's in compliance.

At the pub:

He tried to flirt with the barmaid by explaining how Guinness is made. Clueless wonder.

At a football match:

The clueless wonder cheered when the other team scored. Bless him.

At a restaurant:

She thought "prix fixe" meant you can fix the price. Clueless wonder strikes again.

At home:

He's staring at the boiler like it's about to answer back. Absolute clueless wonder.

VILLAGE IDIOT

Definition: Someone well-known in their community for being stupid or foolish.

At work:

Someone put metal in the office microwave. I'll give you one guess who...our very own village idiot.

At the pub:

The village idiot's dancing on the table again. Must be a Friday.

At a football match:

He tried starting a chant. Got booed by his own side. Village idiot behaviour.

At a restaurant:

He ordered chips, then complained they weren't crisps. Village idiot.

At home:

Who left the front door wide open in January? Oh right, the village idiot did.

NUMBSKULL

Definition: Someone who fails to grasp the obvious; unintelligent.

At work:

The numbskull scheduled two meetings at the same time and invited himself to both.

At the pub:

You spilled three pints trying to carry four, you numbskull.

At a football match:

Only a numbskull waves at the ref asking for a selfie mid-match.

At a restaurant:

She tried to open a bottle of wine with a biro. Numbskull.

At home:

He unplugged the fridge to charge his phone. Utter numbskull.

BLOODY NUISANCE

Definition: Someone or something deeply exasperating.

At work:

The printer never works when you need it to, the thing is a bloody nuisance.

At the pub:

This barstool's been broken for weeks, it's a bloody nuisance.

At a football match:

The bloke sat in front of me is blocking my view of the match. Bloody nuisance, he is.

At a restaurant:

I can barely get any malt vinegar on my chips. This bottle is a bloody nuisance.

At home:

Wash your dish after using it, don't be such a bloody nuisance.

GOBSHITE

Definition: A loudmouthed person who talks nonsense.

At work:

Ignore him. He's just a gobshite who loves hearing himself talk.

At the pub:

That gobshite at the bar won't stop ranting about politics.

With mates:

Don't be a gobshite, mate. You know nothing about football.

At home:

You're acting like a gobshite, shouting about things that don't matter.

In traffic:

Some gobshite's been hooting for ten minutes straight.

KNOBHEAD

Definition: A foolish or annoying person, often oblivious to their behaviour.

At work:

He's a knobhead for taking the last coffee and not refilling the pot.

At the pub:

That knobhead just spilled beer on my jacket.

With mates:

Don't be a knobhead, just admit you were wrong.

In traffic:

What a knobhead, cutting across three lanes with no signal.

At a football match:

The knobhead in front of me is standing up the whole game.

DIV

Definition: An idiot; usually harmless but exasperating.

At work:

He's such a div, forgot to attach the file again.

At the pub:

You're a div for ordering cocktails at a pub.

With mates:

Stop being a div and help me move this sofa.

At home:

You're a div for leaving the fridge open all night.

TOSSER

Definition: A jerk or someone acting in a self-important way.

At the pub:

Don't be such a tosser, just pick a drink already.

At work:

That tosser tried to take credit for my idea.

With mates:

You're being a tosser, showing off like that.

At a football match:

The tosser behind me keeps booing our own team.

On the street:

What a tosser, shouting at everyone for no reason.

MELT

Definition: Someone emotionally soft.

At work:

He's triple checking the printer like it's a NASA rocket ship. Absolute melt.

At the pub:

She ordered a shandy and spilled half of it. What a melt.

At a football match:

Started clapping when the other team scored. Full-on melt behaviour.

At a restaurant:

Sent his steak back because it was "looking at him funny." I mean honestly, what a melt.

At home:

He won't kill a spider but screams for Alexa. Living with a melt.

SILLY SAUSAGE

Definition: Playful and affectionate way to say someone is silly or has made a minor mistake.

At work:

She put the client call on hold and forgot about them. Silly sausage strikes again.

At the pub:

I thought it was karaoke night. It was not. Silly sausage with a mic.

At a football match:

He turned up in a cricket jumper. Bless him, silly sausage.

At a restaurant:

She asked if the "house red" was a paint or a wine. Silly sausage.

At home:

Dad put a sock in the toaster "to warm it up." Can't leave the silly sausage alone for a second.

TART

Definition: Someone who is perceived as promiscuous.

At work:

The new intern's already winking at the boss. Bit of a tart, that one.

At the pub:

Two sips in and she's flirting with the dart board. Classic tart.

At a football match:

Blew a kiss to the striker mid-corner. Tart alert in row C.

At a restaurant:

Ordered dessert before the mains. Total tart move.

At home:

Won't do the dishes unless she's wearing mascara. Honestly...tart.

Insults by Category

Intelligence & Competence

Use these when questioning the wattage of their lightbulb.

NOT THE FULL SHILLING

Definition: A bit off; not quite right.

At home:

He keeps salting his cereal. Not the full shilling, bless him.

At a party:

She brought a tambourine to a dinner party. Not the full shilling, clearly.

At work:

He tried to photocopy his coffee cup. Not the full shilling and HR knows it.

In traffic:

This bloke's parked sideways across three bays. Not the full shilling.

Everyday use:

He calls his plants "Peter" and "Sally." Sweet lad, but not the full shilling.

ONE SANDWICH SHORT OF A PICNIC

Definition: A bit dim, slow on the uptake.

At work:

She tried to email the printer. Definitely one sandwich short of a picnic.

At the pub:

Asked for a "gluten-free pint." One sandwich short, I'm telling you.

At a football match:

Chanted for the ref to get subbed off. He's one sandwich short, that one.

At a restaurant:

Asked the waiter if the duck was vegan. One sandwich short of a picnic.

At home:

Vacuumed the garden. That's not just quirky, that's picnic missing.

ALL MOUTH, NO TROUSERS

Definition: All talk, zero action.

At home:

He promised to fix the boiler last month. All mouth, no trousers.

With mates:

He swore he could sing. One note in, nightmare. All mouth, no trousers.

At work:

She pitched that she'd "revolutionise sales" then ghosted the project. All mouth.

In traffic:

He revved like a maniac at the lights, then stalled. All mouth, no trousers.

At the gym:

He brags about his gym routine while holding a chip butty. All mouth, no trousers.

BRIGHT AS A BLACKOUT

Definition: Thick; the light is on, but nobody is home.

At work:

Asked them to cc the client. They printed the email instead. Bright as a blackout.

At the pub:

He's about as bright as a blackout, he tried to pay for a round with coins.

At a football match:

She spent the whole first half cheering for the wrong team, honestly bright as a blackout.

At a restaurant:

He asked if the sea bass was vegetarian. Bright as a blackout.

At home:

Put the kettle in the fridge and wondered where the milk went. I'm about as bright as a blackout today with everything going on.

DENSE AS DEVON FOG

Definition: Very slow, not the brightest.

In class:

Still asking what page we're on forty minutes in. Dense as Devon fog.

With mates:

He's dense as Devon fog. I explained the joke three times and he's still nodding like it's news.

At home:

She tried to microwave a fork, she's dense as Devon fog.

When driving:

Indicated left, turned right, then asked where they were. Dense as Devon fog.

At the pub:

Took five minutes to realise they were drinking someone else's pint. Dense as Devon fog.

COULDN'T ARGUE THEIR WAY OUT OF A PAPER BAG

Definition: Useless in an argument, with little logic.

At work:

Claimed he deserved the promotion because his rent is increasing. Honestly, couldn't argue his way out of a paper bag.

At the pub:

Got into a debate about VAR and ended up blaming the weather. Paper bag, fully trapped.

At a football match:

Tried arguing with the ref from Row Z, using facts from FIFA 09. Couldn't argue their way out of a paper bag.

At a restaurant:

He complained the steak was too rare, after ordering it blue. Paper bag sealed.

At home:

She insisted the heating wasn't on while sweating through her shirt. Couldn't argue her way out of a paper bag.

BRINGS A SPOON TO A KNIFE FIGHT

Definition: Seriously unprepared.

At work:

Showed up to the pitch with a Canva slide and a smile. Brought a spoon to a knife fight.

At the pub:

Challenged the quiz team, didn't know the capital of France. Spoon.

At a football match:

Turned up in white trainers and a silk scarf. Spoon at a knife fight.

At a restaurant:

Tried to bluff the wine list with "I'll have your reddest red." Spoon.

At home:

He thought assembling IKEA furniture was "intuitive." Spoon, meet Allen key.

Fashion & Appearance

DRESSED IN THE DARK

Definition: So poorly dressed that you can't have had a good look at yourself before leaving the house.

At work:

Shirt inside out, tie looked like an accident. Definitely dressed in the dark.

At the pub:

Bucket hat, Birkenstocks, and a vest...and it wasn't even themed. She dressed in the dark.

At a football match:

Club colours, but not their club. Clearly just grabbed whatever he could in the dark.

At a restaurant:

Sequins at brunch. Dressed in the dark.

At home:

Pyjamas, robe, and socks in sandals. Confidently tragic. Must have dressed in the dark.

BRAVE

Definition: Insane.

At work:

Leopard print trousers and a motivational slogan tee. Brave.

At the pub:

Leather trousers in July. That outfit's brave.

At a football match:

All white kit to an away game. Suicidally brave.

At a restaurant:

Feather boa and elbow gloves. Unless you're the entertainment, brave choice.

At home:

Dressing gown over jeans. Brave. Or mad.

MORE FABRIC THAN TASTE

Definition: When someone's outfit is a crime.

At work:

She's dressed like HR's worst nightmare! More fabric than taste.

At the pub:

It's not a fashion show, mate. More fabric than taste and none of it waterproof.

At a football match:

Dressed like they're presenting the FA Cup, not watching it. More fabric than taste.

At a restaurant:

Silk blouse, feather cuffs...for Nando's? More fabric than taste.

At home:

She just vacuumed in a kaftan. More fabric than taste.

A FACE MADE FOR RADIO

Definition: Unattractive, to put it bluntly.

At work:

He keeps insisting on video calls. Brave, honestly, with a face made for radio.

At the pub:

He got her number in this lighting? Impressive for a face made for radio.

At a football match:

Started a chant and the whole crowd turned. Poor bloke's got a face made for radio.

At a restaurant:

He asked for the romantic corner table. With that face? Made for radio.

At home:

Opened the fridge and it flinched. He's got a face made for radio.

MUST BE LAUNDRY DAY

Definition: Someone's outfit is so ridiculous that it surely must be the last thing in their closet.

At work:

She's wearing last Friday's outfit again. Must be laundry day.

At the pub:

Trackies and a vest top? Bold. Must be laundry day.

At a football match:

That shirt's clinging on for dear life. It must be laundry day.

At a restaurant:

He came to dinner in socks and slides. Must be laundry day.

At home:

Even the dog looked confused by my brother's outfit. It must be laundry day.

Social Etiquette

THAT'S A CHOICE

Definition: When someone makes a choice…the wrong one.

At work:

You told the intern to "own the room," then forgot her name. That was a choice.

At the pub:

Rolling up in white trousers to a Guinness pub? That's a choice.

At a football match:

Please explain why you booed your own keeper. A choice, that.

At a restaurant:

You asked if the chef could "make it taste less French." That was a choice.

At home:

Serving beans on toast for date night? Look, that was a choice.

INTERESTING (OPINION)

Definition: Absolutely mad.

At work:

You think the interns should run the next client pitch? That's an interesting opinion.

At the pub:

Interesting opinion, I wouldn't have thought crying over my ex in the pub was a good way to attract a new girlfriend.

At a football match:

You think we should've let that goal in to make it "fair?" That's an interesting opinion.

At a restaurant:

You reckon ketchup belongs on salmon? Interesting opinion.

At home:

You think Mum and Dad should get matching tattoos? Interesting.

WOULDN'T HAVE SAID THAT OUT LOUD

Definition: When someone lets something slip that they absolutely shouldn't have.

At work:

Telling HR the team's "dead weight?" I wouldn't have said that out loud.

At the pub:

Calling her your "starter wife" on the first date? Wouldn't have said that one out loud.

At a football match:

You shouted that the ref's haircut looks like a hedgehog. I wouldn't have said that out loud myself.

At a restaurant:

Shouting that the potatoes are burnt while the chef's behind you? I wouldn't have said that one out loud.

At home:

Telling Nan she looks 112 years old? I wouldn't have said that out loud.

NOT QUITE...BUT DO GO ON

Definition: You're totally wrong, but I won't stop you.

At work:

You replied-all to correct your boss's grammar? Not quite how I'd have handled it, but go on.

At the pub:

You ordered a rosé and challenged three large men to darts? Not quite what I'd have done, but do go on.

At a football match:

You tried reasoning with a drunken fan...in French? Do go on.

At a restaurant:

You sent back the wine and the waiter? Not quite how I'd have handled it, but go on.

At home:

You told your brother's fiancée she'll "grow on us?" Not quite how I'd have handled it, but go on.

BOLD OF YOU

Definition: Insane. See: "Brave."

At work:

Telling the CEO their business model is weak? A bit bold of you, don't you think?

At the pub:

Wearing white linen and ordering a Guinness? A bit bold of you, don't you think?

At a football match:

He cheered when our striker missed? A bit bold of him, don't you think?

At a restaurant:

Bringing your own hot sauce to a tasting menu? A bit bold of you, don't you think?

At home:

Rearranging the entire living room without telling Mum? A bit bold of you, don't you think?

SOMEONE'S FEELING CONFIDENT

Definition: When someone acts overly self-assured.

At work:

You cc'd the executive team just to show off your colour-coded spreadsheet? Someone's feeling confident today.

At the pub:

He ordered a round before anyone agreed to stay. Someone's feeling confident today.

At a football match:

You turned up in gold trainers and no voice left. Feeling confident today, aren't you?

At a restaurant:

You must be feeling confident, telling the sommelier "Surprise me."

At home:

Dad changed the Wi-Fi name to "Dad Is Always Right?" He's feeling quite confident today.

TAKES A CERTAIN KIND

Definition: When someone has said or done something deemed inappropriate. Used as an assassination of character.

At work:

You called our client's logo "regrettable?" Takes a certain kind of person to say that.

At the pub:

You just asked if the barmaid's "ever seen a dentist." Takes a certain kind.

At a football match:

You clapped when the anthem ended. Takes a certain kind of person.

At a restaurant:

You said the tasting menu "lacks sophistication." Takes a certain kind of person to say that.

At home:

You just called Grandad opinionated. Takes a certain kind.

Cowardice & Hypocrisy

ALL BARK, NO BACKBONE

Definition: Full of big talk, but lacking action, power, or substance.

At work:

He called the presentation "lazy," then showed up unprepared. All bark, no backbone.

At the pub:

Keeps promising to "sort it" next time someone bumps him. All bark, no backbone, mate.

At a football match:

He heckled from behind three rows of stewards. Classic all bark, no backbone energy.

At a restaurant:

Told the waiter the chicken was fine, after complaining it was dry to the table. All bark, no backbone.

At home:

Stormed off during an argument...to mope in the kitchen. All bark, no backbone whatsoever.

STRUTS LIKE THEY OWN THE PLACE, PAYS IN INSTALMENTS

Definition: Someone deeply presumptuous, arrogant, and entirely without merit.

At work:

He struts like he owns the place, barely been here a month.

At the pub:

Ordered a round like a baller, whispered “Split the bill?” two pints in. Pays in instalments.

At a football match:

Front row swagger, nosebleed ticket. Struts like he owns the place, though.

At a restaurant:

Asked for the wine list with bravado, then blinked at the prices. Pays in instalments, clearly.

At home:

They want a Dyson, but pay off the kettle monthly. Strut like they own the place, bless them.

COULDN'T FACE A WET SPONGE

Definition: Someone timid and too weak to confront even the softest challenge.

At work:

Left the room when the intern asked a question. Couldn't face a wet sponge, honestly.

At the pub:

Got loud about "real men," ducked when someone raised a brow. Couldn't face a wet sponge.

At a football match:

Yelled "Fight me" at a pensioner. Changed seats when he stood up. Couldn't face a wet sponge.

At a restaurant:

Critiqued the table service, then flushed when the waiter asked if all was well. Couldn't face a wet sponge.

At home:

Wouldn't confront the spider. Needed backup. Couldn't even face a wet sponge.

EGO WRITES CHEQUES THEY CAN'T CASH

Definition: Someone who talks big but can't back it up.

At work:

Told the team he'd have it "wrapped by lunch." Two days later, still updating the fonts. Ego wrote a cheque.

At the pub:

Bet the whole table he could finish the wings in five minutes. Had a mild cry at wing three. Ego wrote a cheque.

At a football match:

Claimed he could "easily go pro," then tripped during halftime kickabout. Classic overdraft behaviour.

At a restaurant:

Sent back the risotto, said he'd make it better. Can't even boil pasta. Talk about a cheque he can't cash.

At home:

Offered to fix the boiler. Flooded the hallway. Cheque bounced hard.

FIRST TO TALK, LAST TO ACT

Definition: Someone who's full of opinions but mysteriously absent when it's time to deliver.

At work:

Spoke for twenty minutes in the meeting. Didn't send a single follow-up.

At the pub:

Promised a "wild night" and disappeared before round two. First to talk, last to act.

At a football match:

He screamed tactics all match, missed the penalty he took. All talk, last to act.

At a restaurant:

Suggested "family-style sharing," then didn't order anything to share. First to talk, that one.

At home:

He's first to talk, last to act. Said he'd declutter everyone's garbage in the garage. That was three weeks ago. He's still emotionally attached to every Amazon box.

CRUMBLES UNDER EYE CONTACT

Definition: A way of saying someone's confidence is so fragile, even basic human interaction is too much.

At work:

He offered harsh feedback in Slack. Went pink when asked to explain it in person. Crumbled in the first moment.

At the pub:

Mocked someone's shirt, until they turned around. Crumbled like a week-old biscuit.

At a football match:

Taunted the away fans, then hid behind his programme. Crumbled under eye contact.

At a restaurant:

Said "Service is slow" a bit too loud. Waiter stared. He crumbled like a digestive.

At home:

Tried to stand his ground. Eye contact made him apologise in advance. Proper crumbled.

BRAVE ONLINE

Definition: An insult for the keyboard warrior; loud behind a screen, silent in real life.

At work:

Linked to a scathing industry post on LinkedIn. Quiet as a mouse in the office, brave online.

At the pub:

Talks big in the group chat, barely manages "Hi" in real life. Only brave online.

At a football match:

Tweets "Refs are corrupt." Whispers "Sorry" when bumped at the turnstile. Brave online, isn't he?

At a restaurant:

Left a one-star review under "anonymous-foodie87." Got frightened and deleted it a week later. Brave online, that one.

At home:

Posts about "setting boundaries" but can't tell housemates to take the bin out. Brave.

IN LOVE WITH THE SOUND OF THEIR OWN VOICE

Definition: Someone who talks endlessly, convinced they're far more fascinating than they are.

At work:

Started answering a question no one asked. Four slides later, still going. Loves the sound of his own voice.

At the pub:

He's on pint three and anecdote seven. He just loves the sound of his own voice. No one is even listening.

At a football match:

Commentates out loud like it's Sky Sports. Nobody asked, nobody needed. Loves his own voice.

At a restaurant:

Explained the wine pairing. To the waiter. Loves the sound of his own voice.

At home:

Dad asked himself a question, and answered it with a ten-minute story. He just loves the sound of his own voice.

Englishman Mike's Top 100

1. He's not the sharpest knife in the drawer, bless him: more of a butter spreader, really.
2. She's got all the charm of a wet sock and none of the warmth.
3. If he had a thought, it would die of loneliness.
4. She speaks fluent nonsense with just a hint of confidence.
5. I've had more stimulating conversations with my kettle.
6. He walks into a room and the energy leaves.
7. She looks like she gets dressed in the dark during a power cut.
8. He's the human equivalent of beige.
9. I wouldn't trust her to pour the tea, let alone have an opinion.
10. He's got a face for radio and a voice for silent film.
11. I'm sure he tries his best. It just...doesn't show.
12. She's very...consistent. Always wrong, but consistent.
13. Oh no, he's very bright. Like a lighthouse, just not helpful inland.

14. She means well. Pity it never translates.
15. He's not unpleasant, just...surplus to requirements.
16. Her LinkedIn is far more impressive than her actual presence.
17. He has opinions the way pigeons have droppings: frequent, unwelcome, and best avoided.
18. She has that rare ability to make every room colder.
19. He's terribly confident for someone who's wrong so often.
20. He spends a lot of time being loud and wrong in equal measure.
21. If mediocrity were an Olympic sport, she'd be on the podium.
22. He's the sort who'd bring a fork to a soup tasting and act surprised.
23. Her idea of subtlety is using a megaphone in a library.
24. He's not boring, exactly. Just spiritually anaesthetic.
25. She's the kind of person who'd ask for a refund at a funeral.
26. He has the sort of charm that makes you check your wallet after he smiles.
27. She treats common sense like an optional upgrade.
28. He's very impressive on paper. Unfortunately, life isn't lived on paper.

29. I'd say she's out of her depth, but that would imply there's depth to begin with.
30. He strikes me as the kind of person who claps when the plane lands.
31. She thinks being difficult is a personality trait.
32. He's the reason the phrase "with all due respect" exists.
33. She's got a lot of confidence for someone who peaked in Year 9.
34. He has the emotional range of a coat rack.
35. Her presence is felt the way damp is: slowly, unpleasantly, and hard to get rid of.
36. If I wanted her opinion, I'd rattle a tin of biscuits and wait for the noise.
37. He's the kind of colleague who manages to do nothing loudly.
38. She has a special talent for making meetings feel even longer than they are.
39. He says a lot without ever contributing anything.
40. She brings the sort of energy that makes you rethink office friendships entirely.
41. Every time he speaks, a team of brain cells volunteer for retirement.
42. She proofreads emails like she's being paid *not* to.
43. He's the reason HR has a wine budget.

44. If there were an award for being present yet useless, she'd have built a shelf by now.

45. He's the human version of a "low battery" warning.

46. She's the sort of woman who'd tell you off for breathing too loudly.

47. He's a relic from an era no one's nostalgic for.

48. She has all the warmth of a tax return.

49. He's not so much stuck in his ways as fossilised.

50. I've had more engaging chats with my GPS, and it gets lost less often.

51. You're not stupid. You're just very committed to being wrong.

52. You have something no one can take from you: your ignorance.

53. Oh, I'd never call you delusional. That would imply you're imaginative.

54. You have such a brave relationship with self-awareness.

55. You always know exactly what not to say.

56. You must be exhausted from being this wrong all the time.

57. If mediocrity were an Olympic sport, you'd podium every year.

58. You have the charisma of damp cardboard and the insight to match.

59. You've mistaken attention for admiration again, haven't you?

60. Even silence would find you awkward.

61. You're what happens when confidence outpaces competence.

62. You have the unique ability to make anything worse.

63. You add so little, it's impressive how present you insist on being.

64. You're not the main character. You're barely a coherent subplot.

65. If I wanted to hear nonsense, I'd call customer service.

66. There's nothing wrong with being average. You just really commit to it.

67. You manage to be both loud and forgettable. A rare talent.

68. You could start a fight in an empty room and still lose.

69. You've mistaken having the floor for having something to say.

70. You don't need enemies. You've got yourself, and that's plenty.

71. You're the reason people lose faith in education.

72. I've had more stimulating conversations with the toaster.

73. I'd call you a pill, but pills are useful.

74. You look like you lost an argument with a mirror.

75. You make beige seem vibrant.
76. You're not ahead of the curve. You're barely clinging to the graph.
77. You're all volume and no value.
78. You're not stupid, you just have bad luck thinking.
79. You bring everyone so much joy...when you leave the room.
80. You're the reason they put instructions on shampoo bottles.
81. You're proof that evolution can go in reverse.
82. You're impossible to underestimate.
83. I'd agree with you, but then we'd both be wrong.
84. You should put that on your LinkedIn: "Managed to speak without thinking."
85. If common sense were a currency, you'd be bankrupt.
86. Were you born this irritating or did you take evening classes?
87. You're not entirely useless. You could serve as a bad example.
88. You're the human equivalent of a participation trophy.
89. You're about as sharp as a butter knife at a toddler's tea party.
90. I envy people who haven't met you.
91. Your voice has the range of a dial-up modem.

92. You'd struggle to pour tea out of a teapot with instructions.
93. You're the kind of person who claps when the plane lands.
94. You have something no one else has: standards this low.
95. You've got all the charm of a Monday morning.
96. You're living proof that confidence is a scam.
97. You're not a complete idiot. Some parts are missing.
98. You're as useless as the 'g' in lasagna.
99. You're about as sharp as a marble.
100. You're not aging like fine wine. More like milk.

CONCLUSION

How to Wield This New Power

Now that you know how to craft the perfect insult, deliver it with style, and reciprocate with flair, it's time for the final lesson: You've got the knife, now learn to sheathe it. The art of the insult isn't just in lashing out, it's in choosing not to. It's in knowing your audience, reading the room, and acting accordingly. Not every insult is for everyone, and not every moment is appropriate. Always practice restraint. Restraint breeds mystery, and mystery breeds control. The goal, on the surface, is entertainment. When we look deeper, it's also about power. Power to own the room, move the energy, and always come out on top. Understand that if you're always firing, no one fears the bullet. Is it all a bit Machiavellian? Undoubtedly. But true all the same.

Before you go spraying insults like champagne, consider the following: not every target is fair game. Be wary of where, and on whom, you deploy these tactics. Thinking of clapping back in the workplace? Think again. A few things to note in the office specifically: Never insult a subordinate. It is unprofessional at best, and downright cruel at worst.

Understand the power dynamics of the office. When working with a direct report, keep criticism constructive—no jabs, no fun, just feedback! Never insult upwards. That's called unemployment. If you must insult at work, do so sparingly, subtly, and only when absolutely merited. Insults don't exist in a vacuum. Throwing them around recklessly is not witty, it's deeply unwise. Always read the room before speaking. The same line used in two different environments can either charm everyone, or ruin your reputation and alienate you from the group. Boardroom? Pub? Family dinner? Adjust accordingly. Wasting your wit on the wrong audience cheapens it. Sometimes the most worthwhile insult is simply walking away from a situation that is not worth your time.

Use what you've learned here with humour, with intelligence, with kindness, and with good intentions. Have fun with it all! You're not trying to wound anyone, but simply to bring a little bit of wit to a world that sorely needs it. I'll leave you with this: if you must draw blood, do so wisely...and be sure you've mapped the exits. Now off you go, insult your heart out!

About the Author

Michael Baker is an old-school British gentleman in a modern world: sharp-witted, dry as a bone, and allergic to nonsense. A lifelong observer, he turns the unspoken rules of life into an art form, saying what others only dare think. His commentary blends cultural pride with a gift for blunt honesty, delivering not just etiquette, but the psychology behind it.

His work is a testament to the civility and understated humour that defines Britain. He is a devoted husband, proud father to three daughters, and grandfather to a tiny chihuahua, Beluga (like the caviar, not the whale). Most days, you'll find him in a jumper, tea in hand, quietly hoping you don't sit in his favourite chair.

Mango Publishing, established in 2014, publishes an eclectic list of books by diverse authors—both new and established voices—on topics ranging from business, personal growth, women's empowerment, LGBTQ studies, health, and spirituality to history, popular culture, time management, decluttering, lifestyle, mental wellness, aging, and sustainable living. We were named 2019 *and* 2020's #1 fastest growing independent publisher by *Publishers Weekly*. Our success is driven by our main goal, which is to publish high-quality books that will entertain readers as well as make a positive difference in their lives.

Our readers are our most important resource; we value your input, suggestions, and ideas. We'd love to hear from you—after all, we are publishing books for you!

Please stay in touch with us and follow us at:

Facebook: Mango Publishing
Twitter: @MangoPublishing
Instagram: @MangoPublishing
LinkedIn: Mango Publishing
Pinterest: Mango Publishing
Newsletter: mangopublishinggroup.com/newsletter

Join us on Mango's journey to reinvent publishing, one book at a time.

www.ingramcontent.com/pod-product-compliance
Lightning Source LLC
Jackson TN
JSHW032028261025
92296JS00001BA/1

* 9 7 8 1 6 8 4 8 1 8 7 1 6 *